Man Child

by

Holbrook Breckenridge

RoseDog Books
PITTSBURGH, PENNSYLVANIA 15238

RoseDog Books
585 Alpha Drive, Suite 103
Pittsburgh, PA 15238
Visit our website at *www.rosedogbookstore.com*

ISBN: 978-1-6453-0510-1
eISBN: 978-1-6453-0502-6

Dedication

This book has been dedicated in loving memory to my fallen mother, Kalena. She was always my rock, paper, and scissors. She was the first to tell me to cut it out, the one to endure the day in and day out grind to ensure that I had a sense of self and always first to step up to sacrifice so much more than a monetary value. Truly, my lost world.

Man
Child

Chapter One
Taking the approach

The reality that every action gives way to a reaction which determines the next action is a cause-effect relationship that incorporates all of one's life from within and from without.

There will always be three main personality types that each of us will fall into. The three personality types most associated with people include the conformist, the non-conformist, and the innovators. The one common thread that they all have is their unwavering desire to succumb to their aspirations of becoming game changers within the game of life. Our beliefs, attitudes, and opinions can all be changed with the input or extraction of information and/or emotion. Our opinions are the easiest for us to change with the input of more information. Our attitudes are a bit harder to change than our opinions since they evoke emotion; and our beliefs are the hardest to change since they have been positively or negatively reinforced from the onset of our personalities being developed from zero to six years of age.

Communication will forever be the most essential ingredient for progress. Poor communication can lead to a downward spiral of conflict, and it is only through growth, time, and experience that conflicts can be rectified and resolved through stages of denial, anger, grief, and finally acceptance. Only after acceptance is achieved is one truly able to move on to what's next. Every time one grows to acceptance, their experience gains more wisdom which brings about better understanding and appreciation in the progression of growth for gaining more clarity of who we are and what it is that we aspire to achieve.

When attempting to understand ourselves in relation to the universe as a whole, the following concept may prove to be helpful. Taking a two-liter bottle filled with sand and then smashing it on a hard surface will naturally bring about total disorganization. When examining this in relation to the big bang theory and the organization of our solar system; is it so hard to believe that our organized solar system very well came from a disorganized force when taking into account how opposites attract.

In attempting to grasp the cycle of life, the relevance of one's life may very well be as follows. In looking at the innocence yet disorganization of a newborn, then developing into the perfectionist of an adult, only to digress back to disorganization and innocence upon death, there may very well be the method in the madness. Involvement gives way to isolation and isolation gives way to involvement and the primary connecting tissue consist of both space and time, which exist in both life and death. This is what I would describe as a universal cyclical cycle.

In the midst of writing *Mindful Survival*, a family incident occurred. At the time I was living with my sixty-nine year old mother and my twenty-one year old niece who was trying to convince her grandmother to install security cameras on the outside of her property. My mother, being on a tight budget; told my niece that she only wanted one camera over the front door and one camera by the back carport facing the back door of her home. My niece said no; there are going to be two cameras by the front door, two cameras on the side of the house, and two cameras by the back carport multiplying the amount of cameras. Upon hearing this and knowing that my mother owned the home and not my niece; I couldn't help but ask my niece, who is paying for this, a hint that this is your grandmother's house and not yours, for it's not up to you what she chooses to do with it. A confrontation ensued upon going into the house and as she pushed me down and upon my getting up; she sucker punched me in my left front tooth, cracking the enamel into the dentin, and busting the left side of my top lip. As a reaction, I swung my hand around to my mouth and subsequently her left eye was hit and as a result she screamed bloody murder upon calling and telling her mom that I hit her.

My sister showed up and began arguing with me on behalf of her daughter when the police showed up and she painted me in a bad light in front of the police before the investigation had begun. The investigating officer fell for this under handed tactic which compromised the entire investigation, and they allowed my niece to press charges on me; whereby, I got assaulted in jail, mugshot, and finger-printed to be allowed to walk three miles home in the rain in the early hours of the following morning.

Arriving at home, I found my niece had packed her stuff and left while my mother was completely distraught. My mother said she wanted to testify in court with regards to this entire situation on my behalf. It took six months for the court date to arrive, and the night before court, a second incident occurred. Due to the severity involved with regards to the reasoning of going to court in the first place; as well as my mother's upcoming testimony at hand; the sworn testi-mony oath became the issue. You see my mother being sixty-nine years old at the time could not remember word for word what my sister said in reference to tainting the investigation six months prior and with regards to the sworn testimony oath; to the best of your rec-ollection appears to be missing. As a result a felony cruelty to the in-firmed charge came about after I did the wrong thing for the right reason in trying to save her from going to jail. Both charges were eventually dropped and this became a closed case after I did my time; however, this is nevertheless an example of a snowballing effect of how good intentions can be easily misinterpreted, and how crucial communication truly is.

It's such a shame when something built on love falls apart be-cause of love. I find this takes place mostly because of internal per-sonal expectations and demands that are brought about by inflictions that can bring about a spiraling effect which can lead to one's own demise. Intelligent men have successful families if, and only if, they can refrain from trying to buy their love. The same truth applies to women. Love, just like time, has an inherently innate ability to endure. It can't be bought or sold, only passed around within the realm of time and space. Like a dog that chases its tail; the constant circling effect of the quest without the completed satisfaction of victory, is a never ending story. In dealing with desires and the reality that they have desires of their own; it is advantageous to incorporate discipline when considering the importance of being reasonable to one's self and others for no other reason than one's own personal integrity and perseverance to ensure that persons' staying power.

Regarding life and death, the endurance of both is like a clock on the wall constantly accounting for itself destroying itself along fates never ending journey of progress. Time remains constant in life and death which gives way to a premise that consist of two opposites remaining close by way of a neutral party. One example is an atom. Time will forever be in a constant state of neutrality. No one owns it. Therefore no one can waste it. You can not get rid of what you do not possess. You can only go along for the ride whether the ride is positive and/or negative and perseverance is never to be underestimated for the sake of not underestimating your own ability. Remaining grounded is of utmost importance. Once someone reaches the brink of death, their instincts completely take over due to their predicament being beyond any logical rationale of their personal understanding that they themselves can objectively rectify.

Their physical, emotional, and psychological state is totally compromised and is beyond them. Infinity is what I describe as the flat line of time, and in this moment it stands still. Their fate is no longer in their hands, and they have absolutely no control in regards to their destiny.

Regarding the similarities of just how interconnected we truly are this next concept may very well be worth pondering on. Common sense is the intersection between ones beliefs and ones spirituality. The positive and negative reinforcement of ones personality by way of ones beliefs, attitudes, and opinions over time is what gives way to what one is as well as the internal and external role one plays within the realm of one's self and the world around him. This is what gives way to what one does or doesn't believe in regards to a higher power and yes there is power in both positive and negative thinking. The perception of how a person perceives themselves in regards to any circumstance they may find themselves in regarding life; when looking at life as a dream, it may very well be that we are just a figment of someone else's imagination. The same premise holds true with regards to success. This is only the intersection between preparation and opportunity. We all receive a certain number of opportunities in life, and only the opportunities that we are prepared for will we be successful at; whether positive or negative which unequivocally makes us a success in our own right.

When the heart stops, blood is no longer pumped throughout the body. Blood flow stops and circulation ceases to circumvent. The blood throughout the body and brain become oxygen deprived, stagnant, and results in clot. Death becomes imminent due to the accepting stage of exhaustion which gives way to one's final resort to cease and desist. The body-mind connection is what makes our connections with direction possible with regards to either positive or negative reinforcement in either moving forward in the progression of growth or the back slide of a set back in reference to a relapse. The only true continuum when taking these two extremes into account is the consideration of time and space. Like a bird in flight, wren is no more than the tilting of wings. The importance of what one has is not nearly as important as what one does with what one has in regards to either a progression or a setback in moving forward along the road of one's fate. Existence exists and is maintained by the offsetness of non-existence and vice versa. Moderation is what gives way to balance. An enigma, wrapped in a conundrum sealed in an entity, and tucked under a deity of perseverance and fate.

In terms of attitude and behavior, one can easily say "I do not work for you; I work because of you. If I rebel it's in spite of you. If I have done a good job, do not discount my own self satisfaction in knowing that you are satisfied." This is no more than the essence of cooperation that can be seen in either a positive or negative light depending on one's perception. If you are going to be miserable; you are better off being rich than poor, however, no matter how much you have, when it comes to you're personal satisfaction and contentment; the understanding that there are things in life that are priceless is a given. This is no different than having two different animals from the same bloodline all wrapped into one; like a wolf-Rottweiler hybrid. In terms of ownership, the truth remains that you can always acquire more; nevertheless, what you have is still all you've got.

The Chinese symbol that defines the essence of balance that can be used internally as well as externally is that of the yin yang. This symbol cries out more than ever that what you oppose most lives right in the center of you. One that is full of opposition is the one who is least content. The spark of the emotion to oppose mainly stems from unresolved internal issues that have not been addressed on one's personal level. If the issues were, there would be no spark of opposition and contentment would naturally endure.

The harsh truth is that we all are living within the vaccum of space and time and the best we can do is make the best of it within the confines of acceptance that we are all limited to, and enhanced by, with regards to the personal circumstances we each experience from within as well as from without on a day by day basis. The best we can do is the best we can with the abilities we each have knowing and understanding that we will never achieve the most high level of being the designer of all that is, has been, and forever will be; however, the success of living within the realm of our own existence is not too bad when it comes to this fact which encompasses the truth being that life is a success in its own right.

Chapter Two
The Assent

With regards to observational perception and personal stereotypes, it is easy to fall prey to every day incidental conflicts that lead to such belittlement that naturally escalates such situations. The unrelenting truth that no one knows one thing about everything nor everything about one thing, enables each of us to be on a life long journey to seek out personal understanding in our own insatiable thirst for knowledge. There is a personal satisfaction which is temporarily achieved with acquiring different levels of knowledge to validate one's personal understanding of their own wisdom. It is our knowledge, understanding, and wisdom that brings about our self confidence that can have a profound effect on our ability to perceive the future in either a positive or negative light depending on our perception.

Personal insight is the determining factor within the concept of any and all judgment calls made on a daily basis to insure the degrees of survival that we each endure along the road of life. Like a worker whose job is only as good as the tools in his tool box; the more tools acquired by someone for the benefit of one's resources for survival, the greater the chance of one's staying power. Understanding that there is nothing guaranteed in life; it very well may be extremely advantageous to hedge one's bet as much as possible when contemplating the clichés such as the greater the risk, the greater the reward; and how scared money doesn't make money. Both of these clichés encompass another example of two different animals connected by the same bloodline of success.

Referencing the blood make-up of an individual in terms of relevance on a genealogical perspective, with regards to enhancing a person's connection with direction, it becomes extremely difficult to know where a person is going without the knowledge of knowing where they have been. The upside of surviving an identity crisis is the ability to reinvent yourself into anything that you choose to be. This is what I would classify as the epitome of freedom on a personal level, and when applied it becomes easy to comprehend how small the world is, and being limitless can give way to great creativity. At this juncture, the sky is not even the limit, yet it should be well noted with regards to safety, security, stability, and solidarity; how care, truth, choice, trust, chance, try, change, and time should all be taken into consideration; for all are equally relevant.

Simply put, care enough to tell the truth for safety. Make the choice to trust for security. Take the chance to try for stability and change over time for solidarity. Going backwards; you achieve solidarity over time as you change to bring about stability as you try through taking chances to ensure security as you trust your choices to enable safety by telling the truth because you care. This is a philosophical concept that anyone can incorporate into their lifestyle for their own enhancement and personal growth.

When observing life as a hurdle race, it is easy for the one that has never jumped over a hurdle to see the hurdle as an obstacle as opposed to the one that has cleared many hurdles, and sees the next one as a challenge. Being cautiously optimistic is practical and only comes with experience, for some get coal for Christmas and some experience Christmas year round. Realizing life is a two way street and appreciating a personal relationship with yourself and then reach out from within; alleviates much pain and anguish that can stem from expecting the outside world to complete the inner most intricacies of you. Simply put, you can only give what you have already acquired.

Taking the cycle of life into account in dealing with the undeniable truth that history repeats itself, the wise cliché that states that there is nothing new under the sun gives credence when objectively looking at the correlation between life and death. This correlation shows how there is more to life than death and how there is more to death than life. Simply put, when a child arrives or someone dies the factual truth remains that they are not the first, nor will they be the last, when observing this universal cycle for what it is as a whole. Since we only have so much energy; I cannot help but question the reasoning in wasting it on trivial, bitter, and pointless conflicts when such energy when conserved can be used in a much more productive and conducive manner that can be beneficial to oneself and society as a whole on a much greater scale. The sad irony remains; however, that most people only realize what they want in life only after they have received enough of what they don't want. This incorporates the truth of how the acquisition of knowledge stems from a trial and error process that succumbs to personal experience that always gives way to a personal level of wisdom that surfaces naturally as an inherent ability over time.

Upon trying to solve the personal responsibly of an insecurity that may easily give way to trust issues; it is important to recognize the role that one plays in regards to themselves in seeking out the issue of self trust and how stable one is on such a level with regards to allowing such an issue to flow in a conducive manner from the inside out. This begins with a personal level of care, and extends throughout ones philosophical nature until it rest easily on one's belief of solidarity or on a co-operational level. Upon achieving such a feat and not withstanding a setback brings about an overall contentment in allowing life to take its course with the personal understanding that there is much in life that is beyond our control. Sometimes there are things that are better left to chance, while other avenues cry out for complete skepticism. The operational balance lies in staying vigilant as well as cautiously optimistic in staying prepared for what may come.

When being stuck in the past as well as day dreaming too much into the future, the present becomes only seen through foggy goggles. The saying "there is no time like the present" incorporates the importance of the here and now. The present is all that is guaranteed and it is only the speculation of the importance of time, and it is this alone that is what warrants the actions associated within the realm of life. The back and forth conundrum of uncertainty is most often than not the root cause of much ambiguity that can lead to a roller-coaster ride that can be perceived as horrendous or exciting depending on your seat. The moral of the story is as cut and dry and as black and white as saying one should never play with fire for there is nothing funny regarding any and all ramifications in dealing with any situation comprised of having a misunderstanding in conjunction with a firearm. In other words, there is an obvious correlation that exists between safety and staying power, security and money, stability and balance, and last but not least solidarity and cooperation. All are dependent on care which brings forth truth, choices that make way for trust, chance which shows how one tries, and change which always involves time and understanding.

Chapter 3
Leveling Off

The exhilaration of what is next to come is equivalent to the experience of what already has, and the connecting correlation involves nothing more than hope. Hope is what enables the ability to dream of greater aspirations to lend itself to greater freedoms in the free flowing ideas of creativity which empowers each of us our own purpose and ability to achieve what otherwise could have easily given way to complete oppression whereby all past, present, and futuristic states may very well have settled within the confines of desperation and despair. In a state where no hope exists and destitution is the only outlet, suicide becomes the most rational decision.

The cliché that God doesn't close one door without opening a window can fundamentally put hope into what on the surface appears to be a hopeless situation. When seeking justice; knowing the truth that God doesn't sleep and doesn't like ugly gives the self satisfying contentment that every dog gets his day. For just as the world turns, what comes around goes around. The same correlation when dealing with life and death exists in knowing if God takes care of the birds during a hurricane, then surely he will take care of his children whether dead or alive. The option to Live in Peace or Rest in Peace will never change the common denominator that peace on either level ultimately prevails, for anything else is just incidental.

It is easy to see occurrences in life as either good or bad and to place blame on any and all situations that go against one's nature. However, in dealing with such a conundrum in looking at the world as a whole in terms of nature, the obvious question still remains. If a volcano erupts, whether people die or not, is it a good thing or a bad thing or is it just what is? If it is just what is and there is nothing new under the sun in reference to the truth of us not being the first and we will not be the last, then would not the reality remain in saying that it is what it has always been? If yes is the answer, then we shall continue to go around and around like a dog that chases his tail on any and all levels for the simple reason of having no choice for the rock that we coexist with does the same.

The belief in Taoism at its core grounds itself in the belief of the unseen order. The unseen order is that of an invisible straight line of a person's predetermined fate from the onset of life until death. Like a line in the sand we start out going to the right of the line (doing the right thing) then crossing over and going to the left of the line (doing the wrong thing) and repeating this pattern down our fates path. Each time as we cross the center, we self justify our actions in our own personal progression of growth and become more centered within ourselves and actions. Once we become one with the line of our predetermined fate, our life ends. Hence the race may very well be just as important if not equal to the finish line.

A driver once came to a stop sign, slowed down, then continued on. A policeman pulled him over and asked him to step out of the vehicle. The driver pleaded how he slowed down for the stop sign so the policeman began to hit him with his baton. The policeman then asked, "Do you want me to slow down or do you want me to stop?"

The unique abilities that are present in each of us give way to our inherent differences. The ability to understand is one of the greatest abilities we can possibly tap into in the aid and quest for bringing all involved together through a cooperative understanding of unity. In dealing with such a task, there are only three fundamental principles to apply: 1) control what is controllable, 2) accept that which is not controllable, and 3) attempt to transform the undesirable into the desirable. Only after this quest has been achieved will perfection reign supreme and the truth that you catch more bees with sugar than you do with salt will always be of utmost importance.

The actual beginning of any journey begins with a blank slate. Just as the painting paints the painter, and the writing writes the writer, so too does it make sense that nothing ventured, nothing gained. When appreciation is at hand at any stage of life for any and all experiences experienced by anyone, the realization that winning within anyone's lifelong experience becomes easily achievable. It is when we excel at being our greatest and most cynical critics that our happiness falls at our own hands. At this stage it becomes vivid how happiness is just another choice, and how it becomes the adjustment of one's perception regarding their personal outlook that very well may determine if any given moment or experience is conducive and favorable, or non-conducive and unfavorable. Once again wren comes to the rescue as the tilting of the wings determines your rise or fall by which any and all adjustments are completely and totally governed from within.

The hunger for fulfillment from the beast within is a hunger we all share. The importance of satisfying one's needs first and foremost is of the utmost importance seeing how one is of no use to anyone else if he is of no use to himself. If you take the ability to be critical and constructively criticize yourself to be the best you can be with the abilities you have, you become front row and center stage at your own transformational show of turning a bad life into that of greatness. The ability to read between the lines and adjust your stance becomes as fluid as water for it naturally becomes natural. This flow becomes conducive in all that you do, and gives way to a more balanced and easier life.

Chapter Four
The Decent

The high mania has subsided, and the revelation after the manic highs become: my God, how did it get so crazy. This turns into a self complex of am I crazy. The seeking out for answers from this question begs for the answer, has anyone else experienced this, and yes is the answer you find.

Such a let down. I mean, I thought that it was only me, that I was special and unique. That somehow it was all about me. The truth is that we all are, and we are all involved in a grandeur scheme of things. Sure it may seem as though we are all puppets, however the co-dependent relationship that the puppet master has with his puppets makes him a puppet by association.

Taking into account how it takes two to tango within the confines of the action reaction correlation, and the truth of how we are both a product of our environment in conjunction with our natural state of being; the realization of whether or not selfishness is better than being selfless becomes the only true question. The answer lies in the balance of the fact that you can only give what you have, and in a dog eat dog world that takes no prisoners with an overlaying overtone that if you don't get yours no one is going to give it to you; being selfish becomes the truest answer between the two.

All we can do is the best we can within our own ability. In terms of the best of the best in reference to a gift on a personal level; the best gift anyone can give someone is the basic appreciation of where someone is in life and how they got there. This is empathy in its purest state which becomes the foundation of personal respect. Just like selfishness, it has to be achieved on a personal level before it can be shared as seeing how you can only give what you have already acquired. Self restraint and self discipline are learned, and through positive and negative reinforcement over time incorporates them into a lifestyle that centers around the philosophy of caring enough to tell the truth for safety, making the choice to trust for security, taking the chance to try for stability and changing over time for solidarity. It is this philosophy that brings out a lifestyle that brings forth the "I" as opposed to the "me" in each of us.

Finding and then keeping in touch with the "I" in you enables one to be more grounded, better balanced, and centrally centered within ourselves for making a higher quality of rational decisions that may need to be made in crossing any bridge or getting over any obstacle in a more conducive and practical approach for achieving one's goal. In doing so, self confidence is built on one's new found understanding and achievement, while acceptance is achieved for the ability to move on to what's next.

At this point one becomes a blank slate and the world once again is his oyster, and the freedom to choose what the next goal will be is there for the taking. The fringe benefit lies in having the wherewithal of knowing the tools to success have already been incorporated. The questions become: how am I feeling, what am I feeling, and what are my feelings telling me to do. Constant calibration is of utmost importance in order to achieve each answer to each question and the knowledge that no one is insignificant is the greatest wisdom for accomplishing these answers. Understanding the premise that people use people everyday based on their abilities will always withstand the test of time, for as long as one has any ability it shall be used.

Referring to sadness it is important to realize that grief happens at different intervals within one's life because of many different circumstances. Death can be quite the lure for escaping such a feeling, but the truth that time and space connect life and death on both levels of consciousness accompanied by the reality that there is nothing new under the sun, including the fact that we are not the first and we will we not be the last, only leaves us the result of being that of just another statistic. One must truly evaluate any and all options and may come to the realization when it comes to life, which is inclusive of death, and honestly ask what option do I really have? The harsh reality that one may come to understand is that it becomes six, and a half dozen the other. Everyone gets scathed and grows whether they choose to or not, for there is just as much pain in growth as there is growth in pain, as all work encompasses a certain level of discomfort and work will always be incorporated in both and vise versa. It then remains how the flat line of time, infinity, is the only concept that has never felt or ever will feel. I see this as the non-pulsing frozen heart.

If home truly is where the heart is, and each of us have our own; in relation to infinity, is it really so hard to fathom how our heart's can turn cold in an instant? Staying young at heart, and being open to love, for some, becomes an enduring line of work that may be too stressful to sustain as inflictions come from within seeing how within has been inflicted upon. Therapeutic hope becomes one's only chance for survival.

At this stage alone time to process and reflect back on who you are now and who you once were becomes essential, and the work only becomes taking time to make a solid connection which will give you a direction in which way to go. This entails solving an identity crisis by gaining a new identity in who you are now at this juncture in your life and living a new and better life based according to your new identity which gives a new direction in which to travel as well as a new purpose for which to live. The asset entails starting fresh with a new slate to choose from with the ability to turn over a new leaf and the greatest thing about it is that it is all on your terms.

While keeping in mind that the heart is not to be neglected in terms of compassion, love, and respect; and if the greatest symbol for unequivocal balance is that of the yin yang, then the relationship between that of the puppet master and his puppets is undeniably correct. It then is only fitting to incorporate the truth that symbolism is stronger than spirituality as a symbol can represent one's spirit, but a spirit can never represent a symbol. The connecting tissue resides in that of a sign. In other words, it is the intersection between one's beliefs and one's spirituality that gives way to one's common sense. It is the understanding of this that brings out your matrimony in reference to yourself and only after one has come to this impasse can one truly understand who he is, and what it is that he chooses to settle for. We all settle; it just becomes for what.

Chapter Five
The Landing

After transcending into a smooth transitional state of being and realizing the ability to achieve a consciousness of being even keel it becomes paramount to incorporate discipline for the retention of one's staying power. The more discipline exhibited, the greater amount of self control one exhibits within the life he chooses to live. The payoff comes in such assets as self discipline, self respect, self worth, self dignity, self confidence, and self love. Gaining so much grants the ability to give back so much more than a monetary value and can be much more rewarding than sentiment. Maintaining a balance between doing too much or too little becomes the ongoing challenge in maintaining all that we do since both extremes can have deadly consequences.

As with the onset or beginning of any new endeavor, the uncertainty that comes only brings forth turbulence until all scenarios of the endeavor have been scrutinized over until no stone is left unturned and the endeavor has reached its final state of accomplishment. Only then is it laid to rest with a feeling of achievement that will endure until the next endeavor begins. This cycle is never-ending and is to be called out so that one may never forget the achievements one has made for the benefit of acquiring tools needed for the turbulent times that are yet to come; nor should the turbulent times be forgotten for making us who we are. Understanding this dynamic is what gives way to balance. Too much of one, and not enough of the other can easily stop the top from spinning.

Like a profit and loss statement, understanding the concept that we are not the first and we will not be the last lets us all know through the duration of time that everything balances out in the end. It is this undeniable truth that cries out the essential importance of living in the present, as opposed to projecting into the future, or dwelling on the past. However, it should be noted that the pleasantries of reminiscing are an enjoyable past time just as having the ability to dream easily gives way to inspiration. The balance within lies in understanding that too much or too little of anything is not good. It is this understanding that helps maintain one's ability to stay grounded within oneself regardless of what may or may not be circling around him.

Being in control of one's self exhibits the greatest amount of discipline one has at any given time and is best kept in check by the realization and truth that a person that has no control controls nothing. This correlates directly with the earlier mentioning that you can only give what you already have in reference to being selfish. One can dissect it every which way from Sunday, yet the truth still remains that if it walks like a duck and quacks like a duck, then it must be a duck.

Having the knowledge that what comes up must come down in regards to a natural law of physics enables the same relationship when applied to any and all states of one's being. The relative factor that will always relate to how high or to how low anything will go, always balances out in the average of its middle ground. In observing this in regards to moderation, being top or bottom heavy makes one less agile and less balanced. In keeping a low center of gravity, one's foundation becomes much more sturdy.

Contemplation is a reality of everyday thinking in the ongoing planning of what might one do, as well as what is the best thing to do, coupled with what should be done. In assessing such decision making opportunities, the greater the connection one has with what one is feeling, what one's feelings are telling him to do, and what one thinks about what one's feelings are telling him to do, enables the greatest insight into achieving the best direction to go in with regards to this connection. One becomes led astray, confused, and bewildered to the point of being broken and lost when such a connection with direction is broken. Going back to the basics and rebuilding from scratch can, however, be a greater attribute in enabling a stronger foundation with greater internal support to build a greater life than otherwise would have never been achieved. As mentioned in MINDFUL SURVIVAL, just as the broken happy home can be better than the unbroken unhappy home, the effort put forth may very well reap its own dividends.

The undying truth that only you have to wake up with yourself, and go to sleep every night with yourself each night, reassures you that ultimately it is you that is left having to justify your own actions to you. No one can run very far from themselves for everything in life comes out in the wash and the chips will always fall where they may. If you do good, you reap good peace of mind, however, if not, you reap high emotional stress, anxiety, restlessness, and behaviors that stick out like a sore thumb. In life it's all there for the taking, I can't help but wonder what will I do, and what can I live with?

Like a two-way mirror, the looking glass self is a concept in psychology of how one sees themselves the way others see them. It is important to note, however, when you compare yourself out to other people, there will always be someone better than you and someone worse than you. When you compare you only to you, it lessens the burden of trying to please anyone other than you. It becomes a new playing field of only you winning for you or you giving in to you, and outside distractions diminish and the only one left to rise or fall is you. The sense of independence greatly increases, after all you are now playing your game of life directly on your terms, and your empowered control becomes immense. Using and constantly keeping in touch with any and all tools associated with a positive outlook without accepting thoughts of grandeur becomes the constant day in and day out struggle to aid in one's staying power, and the understanding that brings about the knowledge and wisdom of how life is a success in its own right gives way to the satisfaction of knowing you have achieved success if for no other reason than the truth that you have lived. The flat line of time incorporates you into being a success in your own right which can be understood in the concept of how we each may very well be granted the right to be legendary seeing how time makes us all legends in our own right.

Understanding the adept correlation between perception and personal happiness, it may be wise in understanding how making the choice to be happy is just as simple as tweaking one's perception in observing a situation in either a negative or positive light. The switch, nevertheless, is on the inside and it is ultimately up to you whether to flip it or not. This is just another example of what one is able to do if they make up their minds for what they desire to achieve.

One Final Thought
Giving the Approach

Addressing our personal me, my, mine syndrome in our instinctual nature of being selfish comes with a self-justifying price of feeling like a scrooge that is entirely too greedy. The total completeness of feeling a sense of justification, empathy, and never forgetting where one comes from lies in one's personal decision to give back. In doing so exonerates any and all guilty feelings and emotions for being so blessed to receive any and all experiences that one has endured whether positive or negative, yet still remains an asset seeing how something will always be better than nothing. This is what keeps me grounded to the point of knowing how high and how low I must fly in the accordance of staying level. In life you come in by yourself and you experience yourself die alone, therefore you should enjoy yourself while you are here. There is no harm in having fun if and only if you can keep yourself in check while keeping in mind that a has been will always be better than a never was along with the understanding that the strength within a man is not determined by his riches, but by his character and his ability to persevere on. In dealing with one's perseverance in relation to being in it for the long haul, the realization becomes evident when one finally understands that the long haul is not that bad when you are hauling ass together.

Biologically from the inception of the sperm entering the egg constant bombardment of stimuli both internally and externally has occurred in each of us. Referencing death and the stoppage of the aforementioned; would it not be something new in terms of just another experience, and if so, is not something better than nothing in relation to experiencing all that is? It very well may be that of a graduating point for passing the test of life and the only rational fear should be that of stage fright, for your legacy and life is left to your family and loved ones to celebrate and your moments in time are forever etched in the flat line of infinity.

Throughout the contemplation and completion of "Mindful Survival" and "Man Child" it became apparent to me how both works transformed my personal growth and understanding about myself and my surroundings to the level of transition that comprised a hunger, if you will, to put forth another thought for both myself and the reader alike, and it is my hopes for your enjoyment of the previous works and the one at hand for the accomplishment of a transitional point. In dealing with the vast array and multiple amounts of negativity that one may experience within the context of one's life that needs to be rectified and addressed before embarking on a much more positive and conducive journey, and looking at it as a pylon that stands as high as all of the negativity within it that has allowed it to expand; the making of a rational decision to cut it at ground level upon coming to the realization that the negativity that is corrupting your life upon which you systematically flip the pylon over as you reinsert it under the ground to allow the ground to act as a transitional point in transcending the negativity into positivity whereby the amount of positive potential in relation to the once negative potential transitions and the sky is not even the limit in terms of how high one can go becomes an understatement.

Contributions Page:

Best regards to the vast array of individuals that have made this book possible. Taking consideration and gratitude into account, the contributions are entirely too great for anyone to repay upon looking at the experience that I have been so blessed to receive. My only hope is for the reader to remain youthful within the aspects of enjoying one's life. At my core I feel that we are all surviving under the same sky and be it as it may that is nevertheless common ground. The common thread that connects life and death is the constant of time and the understanding that in life we have two choices: to Live in Peace or Rest in Peace, either way, Peace prevails.